AFRO-BETS

BOOK OF
SHAPES

written by Margery W. Brown
illustrated by Howard Simpson

A shape is a space enclosed in a line.

Text copyright © 1991, 2000 by Margery Wheeler Brown. Illustrations rendered by Howard Simpson. Copyright © 2000 by Just Us Books, Inc. All rights reserved. AFRO-BETS ® Book of Shapes is published by Just Us Books, Inc. No part of this book may be reproduced or utilized in any form or by any means, electronic or mechanical, including photocopying, recording or by any information storage and retrieval system, without permission in writing from the publisher.

The AFRO-BETS ® Kids were conceived and created by Wade Hudson and Cheryl Willis Hudson. AFRO-BETS® is a registered trademark. Inquiries should be addressed to JUST US BOOKS, INC. 356 Glenwood Avenue, East Orange, NJ 07017. www.justusbooks.com

Printed in Canada Second Edition   Library of Congress Catalog Number: 91-76334   ISBN: 0-940975-58-0

Meet the Shape Family
And have fun with what you find.

This is a **CIRCLE**, round like the moon.

Like the cookies Langston is baking
They will be ready very soon. UM-m-m.

A circle is the shape of balloons kids like.
And circles are wheels on Tura's ten speed bike.

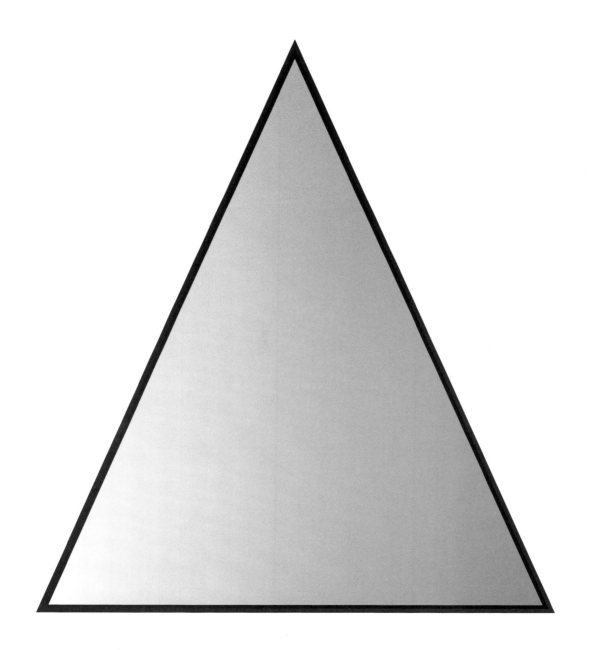

This is a **TRIANGLE**. It has three sides.

Place it on a side and it won't flip,

But someone must help it stand on its tip.

Here is a **SQUARE** with four equal sides.

Big and fancy, or small and plain,

A square's four sides are all the same.

Next, meet a **RECTANGLE**,
With four sides, too.

It might be a box, or a rug on the floor,
A favorite book, or even a door!

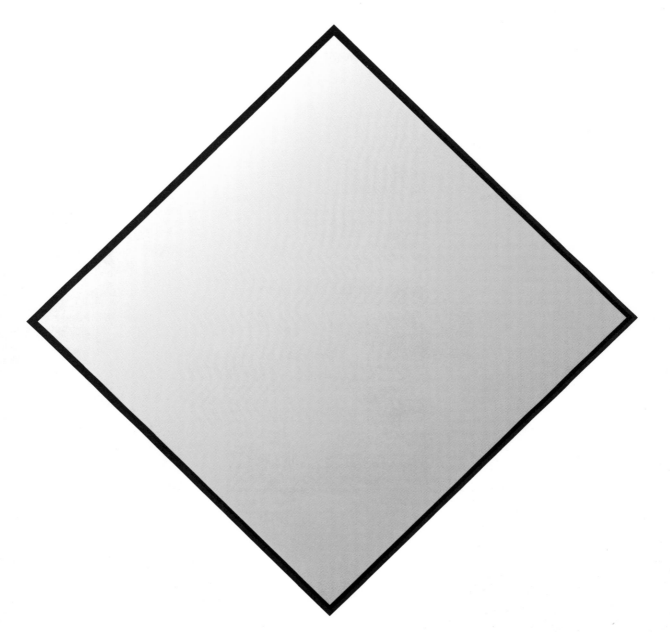

This is a **DIAMOND**.
It has four slanting sides.

It could be the shape of a window pane,
Or the playing field of a baseball game.

It might be a design on Robo's tie,
Or warm sugar cookies for you to try.

Look at the **HEART**, a special shape
With a special meaning, too.

When you give a valentine,

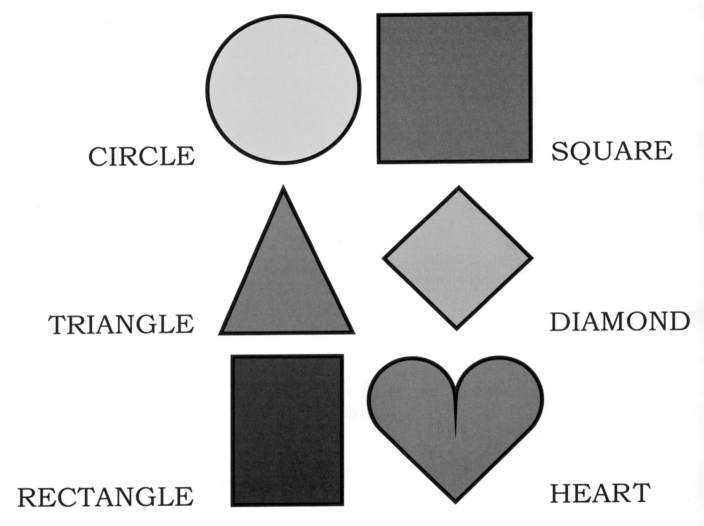

CIRCLE

SQUARE

TRIANGLE

DIAMOND

RECTANGLE

HEART

These six shapes are good to know.
Look for them everywhere you go.
Call each one by its special name,
For no two shapes are just the same.